CIHM/ICMH
Microfiche
Series.

CIHM/ICMH
Collection de
microfiches.

JOURNEY

FROM

FORT PRINCE WALES,

IN HUDSON'S BAY,

TO THE

NORTHERN OCEAN,

FOR THE DISCOVERY OF COPPER MINES AND A NORTH WEST-PASSAGE,

PERFORMED BETWEEN THE YEARS 1769 AND 1772,

BY MR. SAMUEL HEARNE.

PHILADELPHIA:

PRINTED AND SOLD BY JOSEPH & JAMES CRUKSHANK; No. 87, HIGH-STREET.

1802.

JOURNEY

FROM

FORT PRINCE WALES,

TO THE

NORTHERN OCEAN, &c.

THE Hudſon's Bay Company, however, traduced by ſome, as being inimical to diſcoveries within the bounds of their charter, have, on more occaſions than one, ſhewn themſelves zealous in promoting whatever might tend to the honour or benefit of their country, as well as their own individual intereſts.

Animated with thoſe collective views, they appointed Mr. Samuel Hearne, one of their officers, to proſecute diſcoveries in a track little known, even from report of the natives, who ſometimes reſorted to the ſettlement. In his inſtructions, he was directed to proceed towards latitude 70 deg. north, to endeavour to trace the Far-off-Metal River to its mouth, to explore the ſituation of the copper mines, if any, of which indiſtinct accounts had been given; and, in ſhort, to attend to any localities which might be productive of an extended commerce, or geographical knowledge.

His firſt attempt was made in the cloſe of the year 1769, when, after proceeding about two hundred miles, his Indian guides deſerted him; and it was with great difficulty he regained the ſettlement at Fort Prince Wales. Not daunted by this unſucceſsful expedition, he ſet out again on the 23d of February 1770, accompanied by three northern and two ſouthern Indians. Having travelled, without any material occurrence, for upwards of a month, the difficulties of proceeding farther, till the ſeaſon became more advanced, were ſo great that they were induced to pitch their winter tent, in which they lodged till the 27th of April, when they again reſumed their journey.

They reached the river Cathawhachaga, in latitude 63 deg. 4 min. north, about the beginning of July. In their way to the weſtward they croſſed ſeveral other rivers, ſometimes in a canoe, which they carried with them, and ſometimes by fording. As their diſtreſſes multiplied, the Indians again began to ſhew diſſatisfaction; but by an unfortunate accident, on the 11th of Auguſt, the quadrant was broke, at a time when they found themſelves in latitude 63 deg. 10 min. north, longitude 10 deg. 40 min. weſt of Churchill river; and this laid Mr. Hearne under the diſagreeable neceſſity of returning again to the fort. After experiencing incredible diſtreſſes, he reached the ſettlement on the 25th of November, and thus ended his ſecond abortive attempt.

Still reſolute to accompliſh the buſineſs committed to him, and taught by experience how to provide againſt ſeveral ills that he had undergone in his former journeys, Mr. Hearne, with the approbation of the factory, made preparations for a third expedition, which, as it was more intereſting, as well as ſucceſsful, we mean to detail at ſome length.

Having engaged an Indian chief, named Matonabbee, as his guide, who clearly and ſenſibly pointed out the cauſes which had contributed to their former failures, and deſcribed the plan he would wiſh to recommend in this attempt, Mr. Hearne ſet out again, with a party belonging to the Indian chief, on the 7th of December 1770; and for ſome days they found the weather tolerably mild for that ſeaſon of the year.

On the 16th, they arrived at Egg River, where Matonabbee and his friends had ſecured, as they thought, ſome proviſions and neceſſary implements a ſhort time before. On examining the place of the depoſit, however, they found the whole had been carried off by ſome of the Indians, who had paſſed that way; a loſs which was ſeverely felt by them, but borne with heroic fortitude; nor did a word of revenge, in caſe it ſhould be in their power, eſcape their lips.

On the 18th, as they were continuing their courſe, they diſcovered ſeveral joints of deer in good preſervation, which had been recently killed by ſome unknown Indians. On this they feaſted with much ſatisfaction, as they had fared very hard for ſome preceding days. Entering ſome woods on the 26th, they had the good fortune to kill four deer; and as they had not taſted any thing for three days, except a pipe of tobacco and a draught of ſnow water, their ſtrength, loaded as they were, was beginning to fail, and they requeſted leave to halt a day, to refreſh themſelves.

Our author ſays, he never ſpent ſuch a melancholy Chriſtmas in his life; and when he reflected on the delicacies that were then expending in every part of Chriſtendom, under the preſſure of fatigue and hunger, he could not refrain from wiſhing himſelf in a more genial clime. The Indians, however, kept in good ſpirits, and flattered him that they would ſoon find better roads, and deer and game in greater plenty.

Directing their courſe to the weſtward, they entered on thick ſhrubby woods, conſiſting chiefly of ſtunted pines and dwarf junipers, with ſome few willow buſhes and poplars.

On the 30th, they arrived at the eaſt ſide of Iſland Lake, where they killed two large deer. In the evening of that day the guide was taken ill; and from the nature of his complaint, it appeared, that gorging ſome days before was the principal cauſe of it. Nothing is more common, indeed, than for theſe people to overload their ſtomachs after being weakened by long faſting, and the effect of this cannot but be felt. Yet, though they are voluptuaries, when it is in their power, no nation can ſupport longer abſtinence, or ſhew more fortitude under the privation of every neceſſary.

On the 1ſt of January 1771, they proceeded on about ſixteen miles along the ſame lake, when they came to two tents, in which ſome of the wives and families of Matonabbee's party had been left, waiting their huſbands' return from the fort.

Here they found two men, and about twenty women and children; and as thoſe two men had neither gun nor ammunition, they had no other means of ſubſiſting themſelves and friends, but by catching fiſh, and ſnaring a few rabbits. The former were plentiful, and conſiſted of pike, barbel, and trout, with ſome fiſh for which we have no Engliſh name.

The centre of Iſland Lake lies in latitude 60 deg. 45 min. north, longitude 102 deg. 25 min. weſt from London. It is in ſome places about thirty-five miles wide, and is ſo full of iſlands, that the whole lake reſembles a jumble of winding rivers and creeks. Fiſh is abundant in every part, and therefore, it is a favourite ſtation with the northern Indians, who viſit Prince of Wales's Fort in autumn. Many of the iſlands, as well as the main land around the lake, are covered with dwarf wood. The face of the country, like all that to the north of Seal River, is hilly and full of rocks.

Purſuing their journey towards the north-weſt, their proviſions ran very short, till the 16th, when the Indians killed no fewer than twelve deer. This supply induced them to halt a few days, in order to dry and pound some meat, to render it lighter of carriage.

Having, by the 22d, prepared a sufficient stock of portable provisions, and repaired their sledges and snow shoes, they resumed their journey. In the afternoon of that day, they fell in with a stranger who had one of Matonabbee's wives under his care. This was the first person they had seen, in travelling some hundred miles, who was not connected with their own party: a proof how thinly this part of the country was peopled.

Next day they found deer still more numerous; and contragulated themselves on the prospect of suffering no more want during the winter.

On the 3d of February, they were so near the edge of the woods, that the barren land was in sight to the northward; and as the woods trended to the west, they were obliged to [illegible] in their direction, for the sake of keeping among them, and consequently a mong the deer. This day they ſaw ſeveral ſtrangers, ſome of whom joined their party.

On the 6th, they croſſed the main branch of Cathawhachaga River, about three quarters of a mile broad; and ſoon after arrived at the ſide of Partridge Lake, which they croſſed on the ice next day, where it was about fourteen miles over. The intenſity of the cold was beyond expreſſion, and many of the crew were froſt bitten. One of the Matonabbee's wives was ſo frozen, as to be almoſt incruſted on the lower parts with ice; and as ſhe was thawing in great pain, her companions only jeered her, and told her ſhe was rightly ſerved for belting her clothes ſo high; a circumſtance which they aſcribed to the vanity of ſhewing a well-turned leg.

After paſſing Partridge Lake, they found deer ſo abundant for many days, that the Indians killed more than they could eat or carry with them. Accuſtomed themſelves to ſubſiſt on precarious ſupplies, they have no idea of ſaving for the benefit of others; and riot on game when they fall in with it, regardless of real wants, or the future consequences of the devastation they make.

On the 21st, they crossed the Snowbird Lake, and found deer as plentiful as before, so that much time was expended in killing and eating them; but as Mr. Hearne was assured that the season would by no means premit them to proceed in a direct line to the Copper-Mine River, this delay was of little consequence.

In crossing Pike Lake, on the 3d of March, they came up to a large tent of northern Indians, who had been living there from the beginning of winter, and had employed that long interval in catching deer in a pound. Indeed so successful is this method of sporting, in a country where the game is so abundant, that many families subsist by it, without having occasion to move their tents above once or twice in the course of a whole winter.

Such an easy mode of procuring subsistance in the winter months, is a capital blessing to the aged and the infirm;

but is apt to render the young and active indolent and inert; for as thoſe parts of the country, where deer abound, are deſtitute of every animal of the fur kind, it cannot be ſuppoſed that ſuch as can live with ſo little toil, will give themſelves the trouble of hunting for furs, which are requiſite to procure them ammunition and other European commodities. Such is the language, our author obſerves, of the more induſtrious among the indians themſelves; but in his opinion, there cannot exiſt a ſtronger proof, that mankind were not created for happineſs in this world, than the conduct of the miſerable beings who inhabit this wretched part of it*. None but the aged, the infirm, the women, and children, and a few who are regardleſs of opinion (and they are the happy few every where!) will ſubmit to remain in the parts where food and clothing are to

* Man was certainly made for happineſs; but his own fooliſh paſſions, or his being a ſlave to the paſſions or opinions of others, deprive him in every climate of his birth right. From theſe ſources flow the infelicity of man; not that nature has been unkind, or God unjuſt.

be procured on ſuch eaſy terms; be-
cauſe they cannot ſhine as hunters, or accumulate furs. And what do the more induſtrious gain by all their trouble? Their real wants are eaſily ſupplied. A hatchet, an ice chiſſel, a file, and a knife are all that is required to enable them to procure a comfortable livelihood; and thoſe who aim at more, are always the moſt unhappy, and have the moſt numerous wants to ſupply.

Thoſe who bring their furs to the factory, indeed, pride themſelves much on the reſpect which is ſhewn them by the Engliſh; to obtain which, they frequently run the riſk of being ſtarved in their way thither or back; and all they can poſſibly procure for their year's labour, ſeldom amounts to more than is ſufficient to yield a bare ſubſiſtence till the return of the ſeaſon; while ſuch as are deſpiſed for their indolence or want of ſpirit, generally live in a ſtate of plenty; and conſequently muſt be moſt happy and moſt independant alſo. He therefore is at once the greateſt philoſopher and the wiſeſt man, who lives for himſelf, his family, and friends; and laughs at the madneſs of ambition, and the whiſtlings of a name.

Having ſtopped a night in company with the Indians whom they found on the Pike Lake, they began croſſing the remainder of it next morning; but though the weather was fine, and the whole breadth not more than twenty-ſeven miles, the Indians were ſo full of play, that they were upwards of two days before they reached the weſt ſide of it.

On the 8th of March, they lay near a place called Black Bear Hill, where they killed two deer; and next day they had ſuch fine pleaſant weather, as gave them the prelude of ſpring though little thaw was yet viſible.

On the 19th, they ſaw the track of ſeveral ſtrangers; and on the ſubſequent day came up to five tents of northern Indians, who had reſided there great part of the winter, ſnaring deer.

At this place a ſtorm came on which raged with ſuch violence, that they did not move for ſeveral days; and as ſome of the Indians they had fallen in with, were proceeding to Fort Prince Wales, Mr. Hearne embraced the opportunity of ſending a letter by them to the chief, to acquaint him with his progreſs. The latitude here was calculated to be 61 deg. 30 min. north, longitude about 19 deg. 50 min. weſt of Churchill River.

The weather becoming fair and temperate on the 23d, they again purſued their way, and on that and the ſucceeding days, they fell in with ſeveral Indians, ſome of whom being acquaintances of the party, joined company.

Continuing to ſhape their courſe to the weſt-ward, on the 8th of April, they arrived at a lake called Little Fiſh Hill, and pitched their tents on an iſland in it. Here the Indians finding deer very numerous, determined to ſtay ſome time, and to lay in a ſtock of portable proviſions; becauſe, from the ſeaſon of the year, they were aware, that their game would ſoon quit the the covert of the woods for the barren grounds.

At this time the party did not conſiſt of leſs than ſeventy perſons, who were lodged in ſeven tents. For ten days the hunting went on briſkly, and having procured an adequate ſupply of dried ſtores, they again ſet off on the 18th of April. After travelling about ten miles, they came to a tent of Indians, near the Thelewey-aza River. From theſe people Matonabbee purchaſed another wife, though he had ſix before; and moſt of them of the ſize of grenadiers. Indeed the chief pride of an indian is to have a wife of ſtrength rather than beauty; for in a country like this, where a partner, able to endure hard labour, is the chief motive for the union, and the attachment of ſex a ſecondary object, this preference of choice is not to be wondered at.

In general, the women here are far from being objects of attraction, according to our ideas of beauty; though there are a few, when young, that are not quite deſtitute of perſonal charms. Hard labour, however, hard fare, and a rigorous climate, ſoon render them wrinkled; and they have all the marks of decripitute before they are thirty.

But this does not render them leſs dear and valuable to their owners, provided their ſtrength remains; and a woman who can carry eight or ten ſtone weight in ſummer, or drag a much greater weight in winter, is ſure of a huſband, whatever her perſon may be. As for good temper and mental accompliſhments, of ſo much conſequence in poliſhed ſociety, and without which the conjugal union muſt be a ſtate of miſery, it is here of little value. The men have a wonderful facility in making the moſt ſtubborn comply, with as much promptitude as the moſt willing; the command is given, and it muſt be obeyed.

Women indeed are kept at a very great diſtance. They perform the moſt laborious offices; and yet the meaneſt male in the family muſt be ſatisfied before wife or daughter is permited to taſte a bit; and in times of ſcarcity, they frequently go without a ſingle morſel. Should they attempt to ſerve themſelves in ſecret, it muſt be done with great caution, as a detection would ſubject them to a beating at leaſt. Indeed, an embezzlement of provisions would be a blot in their character which it would be difficult to efface.

As the vicinity of Thelewey-aza River afforded plenty of good birch, they halted there several days to complete the wood work for the canoes, and other necessary purposes. On the 20th, a brother of the Indian guide, and some others were sent forward to a small lake, named Clowey, to build a canoe with all expedition.

The children are always named by the parents, or some of their nearest relations. Boys have various appellations, generally derived from place, season, or animal; but the names of the girls are chiefly taken from some part or property of a martin; such as the white martin, the black martin; the martin's head, the martin's tail, &c.

They now shaped their course nearly north; but the snow was so much melted from the heat of the sun, that they were ten days in reaching Clowey, though the distance was not more than eighty-five miles from the last station.

On their arrival at Clowey (a lake about twelve miles over) the 3d of May, they found their captain's brother and associates had only distanced them three days. Here they were joined by several Indians from different quarters, all with an intent of building their canoes at the same place.

It was the 20th before the canoes belonging to Mr. Hearne's party were ready. These vessels are necessarily very slight and simple in their construction, as it is sometimes requisite to carry them more than one hundred miles. Their chief use is to cross lakes and unfordable rivers, after the ice is dissolved; for in winter, both land and water are one solid mass. The Indian employs no other tools in the construction of his vessel, save a hatchet, a knife, a file, and an awl; yet the workmanship is not to be excelled by what the most expert artist could accomplish with every tool in common use.

The shape of the northern Indian canoes bears some resemblance to a weaver's shuttle, but the stern is by far the widest part, as there the baggage is generally laid, and occasionally a second person stretched out at his full length. The dimentions are about twelve feet long, by two in the widest part. The bottom is quite flat. The single paddle is generally used in steering.

Mr. Hearne distributed a little tobacco among the Indians they fell in with at Clowey; and indeed, a pipe or two, and sometimes a present of a few inches of roll tobacco, were always expected by every stranger of any consequence. This constant demand, added to the consumption of his own party, diminished his stores more than one half, before he had proceeded thus far. Gunpowder and shot are likewise articles of high estimation among the Indians; and Matonabbee, from his own supplies, liberally gratified his countrymen with them.

Leaving Clowey, they proceeded northward. Soon after fell in with some strangers, who informed them that Captain Keelshies was within a day's walk to the southward. By this chief, our author had dispatched a letter to the Fort in his last attempt, just before the quadrant was broke; and they had not met since. Two young men were therefore commissioned to proceed to Keelshies station, to receive the letters and goods that had been instrusted to him on Mr. Hearne's account. These returned on the 22d, and reported that Captain Keelshies intended to join them in a few days, and deliver the things with his own hand.

The evening of the 24th of May, the weather was excessively bad, accompanied with violent thunder and lightning. Next morning, however, the wind veering about, it became intensely cold and frosty, which much impeded their progress. The country over which they travelled now, was quite barren, and sprinkled with a few dry stumps of trees.

On the 27th, resuming their journey, they walked about twelve miles to the northward, on the ice of a small river that falls into Peshew Lake. Seeing a smoke to the southward, they advanced to an island in that lake, and there pitched their tents with an intention of waiting the approach of Captain Keelshies.

In the night, one of Matonabbee's wives and another women eloped; and it was supposed they had gone to rejoin their former husbands, from whom they had some time before been taken by force. The chief was almost inconsolable for the loss of his wife, though he had still six remaining. Indeed it seems she was by far the handsomest of his flock, and possessed every valuable and engaging quality to be found in an Indian. She appeared, however, unhappy with Matonabbee; and probably preferred being the sole wife of a young fellow of less note, than to share the divided affection of the greatest man of the country.

Time immemorial, it has been a custom among those people to wrestle for the woman to whom they are attached; and of course, the strongest carries off the prize. Indeed without a considerable share of bodily strength, or some natural or acquired consequence, it is seldom permitted to keep a wife, whom a ſtronger man thinks worth his notice, or whom he wants to aſſiſt in carrying his goods.

This ſavage and unnatural cuſtom prevails throughout all their tribes, and excites a ſpirit of emulation among youth to diſtinguiſh themſelves in gymnaſtic exerciſes, to enable them to protect their wives and property.

The manner in which they tear the women an other property from each otheir, is not ſo much by fighting as by hauling each other by the hair of the head. Seldom any hurt is done in thoſe rencounters. Before the conteſt begins, it is not unuſual for one or both of the combatants to cut of his hair, and to greaſe his ears in private. If one only is ſhorn, though he be the weakeſt man, he generally obtains the victory; ſo that it is evident, addreſs will ever exceed mere ſtrength among all nations.

The by-ſtanders never interfere on theſe occaſions; not even the neareſt relations, except by advice to purſue or abandon the conteſt. Scarcely a day paſſes without ſome overtures being made for contests of this kind; and our author says, it often affected him much, to see the object of the dispute, sitting in pensive silence, and awaiting the termination of the combat, which was to decide her fate. Sometimes a woman happens to be won by a man whom she mortally hates; but even in this case, she must be passive, should she at the same time be torn from a man she really loves.

It is generally, however, young women, or at least such as have no children, who thus frequently change masters; for few are fond of maintaining the children of others, except on parcular occasions.

Some of the aged, particularly if they have the reputation of being conjurers, possess great influence over the rabble, and sometimes prevent such irregularities. As far, indeed, as their own family and connections are concerned, they will exert their utmost influence; but when their own relations are guilty, they seldom interfere. This partial conduct creates them ſecret, as well as open, enemies; but fear or ſuperſtition prevents the ebulitions of revenge.

Unprincipled and ſavage as the northern Indians may appear, in robbing each other, not only of their property, but their wives, they are naturally mild, and ſeldom carry their enmity farther than wreſtling. A murder is ſeldom heard of among them; and the perpetrator of ſuch a horrid crime is ſure to experience the fate of Cain: he is a wanderer, and becomes forlorn and forſaken, even by his own relations and former friends.

Captain Keelſhies joined them on the morning of the 29th. He delivered a packet of letters to Mr. Hearne, and ſuch goods as had been inſtruſted to him, which his own neceſſities, in the intermediate time, had not tempted him to uſe.

He cried often, in ſign of ſorrow, for having been obliged to embezzle ſo much; and as the only recompence then in his power, gave our author ſome ready-dreſſed mooſe ſkins, which were in reality more acceptable, in his preſent ſituation, than what Keelſhies had expended.

Same day an event happened that had nearly put an end to the expedition. An Indian joined them, who inſiſted on taking one of Matonabbee's wives by force, unleſs he gave him a certain quantity of ammunition, iron, and other articles. The man, it appears, had very lately ſold the woman to the captain; but having expended all the purchaſe value, he was determined to make another bargain for her; and as ſhe was a very uſeful woman, and dexterous in every female art, that gained credit among theſe people, the chief was reduced to the moſt mortifying dilemma. He was ſenſible he was not able to wreſtle with the claimant; he was exaſperated at the trick put upon him; however, after ſome hours ſquabbling, the preſents were produced, and the woman remained with Matonabbee.

But this indignity he could not brook; he threatened to renounce his countrymen, and to join the Athapuſco Indians, with whofe chiefs he was well acquainted; and from whom he faid he had always met with more civility than from his own people. Had this refolution been carried into effect, there would have been an end of the expedition to the Copper-Mine River; for the Athapufco country lies in a different direction.

Alamred with the profpect of a third failure, though under no apprehenfion of perfonal fafety, Mr. Hearne waited with anxiety till he thought the paffion of the chief had a little abated; and then by foothing language, by the arguments of duty, intereft and fidelity to the Hudfon's Bay Company, he urged him not to abandon an expedition which could not be carried on without him, and for conducting which to a fortunate iffue, he might expect not only favour, but reward.

Rage at laft fubfided; and the chief, though late in the afternoon, ordered his crew to advance, and after walking fome miles they put up on another ifland in Pefhew Lake.

Having got to the north fide of this lake on the 30th, every arrangement was made for facilitating the execution of the fcheme. Moft of the women and children were to be left under the care of fome Indians, with orders to proceed to the northward at their leifure, and to wait the return of the party from the Copper River, at a place appointed. Matonabbee took only two of his youngeft wives with him, who were lightly laden; and indeed, it was agreed on, that no one in the party fhould carry more ammunition, or other articles, than was abfolutely neceffary for the occafion.

The women expreffed great forrow at parting, and the chief was obliged to ufe all his authority to keep his part of them from following him. Their yells were moft peteous, as long as they were within hearing; while the indians walked on with a gay indifference, feldom thinking of thofe they left behind, or confining their whole regard to their younger children.

They were now in lattitude 64, so that they saw as well to walk or hunt by night as by day. Here they found a few deer, though this kind of game had long ceased to be plentiful, and they had chiefly subsisted on their dried provisions.

It should have been observed, that a number of Indians joined them at Clowey, and intended to accompany them to the Copper-Mine River, with no other object than to murder the Esquimaux, who, they understood, frequented that river in considerable numbers. This horrid scheme, it seems, was universally approved of, and every man equipped himself with a target, before he left the woods of Clowey. Nevertheless, when the women and children were about to be left, only sixty volunteers followed Matonabbee's party; the rest more prudently staid with their wives and families.

As soon as Mr. Hearne was apprized of this barbarous intention, of murdering a people who had done them no injury, he zealously strove to dissuade them from ſuch a deſign; but ſo far were his entreaties from being regarded, they apprehended he was actuated by cowardice and with many marks of deriſion, told him, he was afraid of the Eſquimaux. Knowing his perſonal ſafety depended on the ideas his attendants formed of his courage, he was obliged to change his tone, and affected the hero. He found it in vain, indeed, to attempt to ſtem the torrent of ſavage prejudice, or to inſpire more humane or juſt principles, and therefore he in future left them to their own diſcretion.

Being now exonerated from every uſeleſs encumberance or cauſe of delay, they purſued their journey to the northward with great ſpeed; but, owing to the badneſs of the weather, it was the middle of June before they reached the latitude of 67 deg. 30 min.

In their way thither, they croſſed ſeveral lakes on the ice: and in ſome creeks and rivers they caught a few fiſh. Deer were ſo plentiful, that the Indians killed numbers merely for the fat, marrow and tongues; nor was it poſſible to make them desist from this unnecessary destruction of the poor animals. They insisted on it, that killing plenty of deer or other game in one season, would never make them scarce in another; and when it was in their power to live on the best, it would be folly to neglect it. Such are the narrow, selfish views of people who are destitute of elegancies, and who, at best, have the means of no more than a precarious subsistence.

Having passed Cogead Lake, on the 20th of June, on the ice, the following day they were surrounded by such a thick fog, that they could not see their way. However, in a few hours, the sun broke out, and did not set at all; a convincing proof that they were then within the arctic polar circle.

On the 22d, they arrived at a branch of Congecathawhachaga River; and as the ice was now broken up, they passed it in their canoes, with the friendly assistance of some Copper Indians, whom they found on its banks, employed in killing deer.

Matonabbee, and many of his countrymen, were perſonably acquainted with moſt of thoſe Copper Indians; and their meeting was highly greatful to both parties. A feaſt of dried meat and fat was prepared, and Matonabbee and his friends were invited to partake of it.

The Copper Indians being made acquainted with the object of the preſent journey, highly approved of it, and even offered their aſſiſtance, particularly in lending their canoes, which they ſaid would be very uſeful during the remainder of the journey. Our author, according to his inſtructons, ſmoked the calumet of peace with the principal of the Copper Indians, who was delighted with the proſpect of a ſettlement in his country; and ſeemed to think there could be no impediment to prevent it; for though he acknowledged that he had never ſeen the ſea clear of ice at the mouth of the Copper River, yet it did not occur to him, that this muſt prevent ſhips from approaching their territories.

The whole party of the Copper Indians, notwithſtanding they had never ſeen an Engliſhman before, were extremely civil and obliging; our traveller made them a preſent of ſome ſuch articles as he had, to conciliate their affection the more. They pronounced him to be a perfect human being, except in the colour of his hair and eyes; the former they ſaid was like the ſtained hair of a buffaloe's tail; and the latter like thoſe of a gull. The whiteneſs of his ſkin they thought no ornament; and compared it to fleſh ſodden in water. However, he was conſidered as a great curioſity, and treated with much reſpect. When he combed his head, they aſked for the hairs that came off, which they carefully wrapped up, ſaying, "when I ſee you again, you ſhall ſee this." Hence it ſeems, that among the civilized and uncivilized, a lock of hair is regarded as a proof of affection, or as a memorial of friendſhip.

Matonabbee now diſpatched his brother and ſeveral Copper Indians, to Copper-Mine River, to announce the arrival of the ſtrangers, and the objects they had in view; and that they might meet with a more welcome reception, tobacco and otheir trifling articles were were ſent by the ſame conveyance, to be diſtributed in preſents.

As it was reſolved on to leave all the women at this place, and to proceed to the Copper-Mine River without them, it was neceſſary to continue here a few days to kill deer ſufficient for their ſupport, during the period of abſence. Though game was moſt abundant, ſo large was the daily conſumption, that it was ſome time before they could procure adequate ſupply for the women and for themſelves. Meat, cut in thin ſlices and dried, is not only very portable but palatable; and, with care to air it during the hot weather, will keep for a year without injury.

Notwithſtanding the hoſpitable manner in which the Copper Indians behaved, in ſpite of Matonabbee's exertions, ſome of his party made free with their young women, clothes and bows; a circumſtance very diſtreſſing to our author. The chief, indeed, did not ſeem to think there was much harm in monopolizing the women; but he endeavoured to repreſs the depredations of his followers on other kinds of property, without making a due equivalent.

That a plurality of wives ſhould be the univerſal cuſtom among theſe tribes, is not much to be wondered at, when it is conſidered that they are the greateſt travellers on earth; and as they have neither beaſt of burden or water carriage, every good hunter is under the neceſſity of having perſons to carry his furs to market; and none are ſo well adapted for this work as the women, who are inured to carry and haul heavy goods from their very childhood; ſo that he who is capable of providing for three, four, or more women, is, comparatively ſpeaking, a great man. Jealouſies however ſometimes appear among them, notwithſtanding habit has familiarized them to their ſituation; but as the huſband is always arbitrator, the diſputes are ſoon ſettled, and ſubmiſſion muſt be paid to his commands,

The northern Indian women are the mildeſt and moſt virtuous of the North

American natives; while the ſouthern Indian females are remarkable for the diſſoluteneſs and indecency of their manners. In fact, they are ſo far from laying any reſtraints on the appetites and paſſions, that they indulge themſelves in all the groſſneſs of ſenſuality, and even of inceſtuous debauchery. No accompliſhments whatever, in man, can conciliate their affections, or preſerve their chaſtity.

But though the northern Indian women are incomparably the moſt virtuous, it is no unuſual thing for their huſbands to exchange beds with each other for a night. This, however, brings no diſgrace; but, on the contrary, is conſidered as the ſtrongeſt cement of friendſhip between families; and in each caſe of the death of either of the men, the other thinks himſelf bound to ſupport the children of the deceaſed, and is never known to ſwerve from the duty of a parent. Thus we ſee how nearly virtues and vices are allied.

Though the northern Indians make no ſcruple of having two or three ſiſters for wives at the ſame time; yet they are very particular in obſerving a proper diſtance in the conſanguinity of thoſe whom they admit to their beds. The ſouthern Indians, however, follow the moſt inceſtuous practices, without any ſenſe of impropriety.

By the 1ſt of July, they were ready to proceed on their journey; and having determined the latitude of Congecathawhachaga to be 68 deg. 46 min. north, and long. 118 deg. 15 min. weſt. from London, they ſet out. At firſt the weather was extremely unpropitious, and they made little progreſs. on the 4th it became more temperate, and they walked over the Snowy Mountains, as they are called. At a diſtance, they reſemble a confuſed heap of ſtones, utterly impaſſable; but under the guidance of the Copper Indians, who knew the beſt track, they paſſed them, though not without being obliged to crawl ſometimes on their hands and knees.

By the ſide of the path, in ſeveral places, were large flat ſtones, covered with many thouſands of ſmall pebbles, which the Copper Indians informed them had been gradually collected by paſſengers going to and from the mines. Of courſe they added to the heap.

As the ſnow, ſleet, and rain, fell without intermiſſion on the 5th, they halted; but next day they were able to advance about eleven miles to the north-weſt. Perceiving, however, the approach of a ſtorm, they looked out for ſhelter among the rocks, as they had done the four preceding nights; having neither tents nor poles to erect them with.

Next morning ſeveral of the volunteers deſerted them, being quite ſick of the hardſhips they endured. For ſome days they had not been a moment dry; even at night, the water was conſtantly dropping from the rocks that hung over them, and formed their ſole ſhelter from the inclemency of the weather. Except to light their pipes, it was impoſſible to kindle any fire.

Early on the morning of the 7th, they crawled from their receſſes, and as the ſun was hot, it ſoon melted the recent ſnow; and towards night they reached Muſk Ox Lake, ſo called from the number of thoſe animals they found on its margin. The Indians killed ſeveral of them; but as the fleſh was lean, they only ſtripped the bulls for the ſake of their hides.

This was the firſt time they had ſeen any of thoſe animals, ſince they left the factory. In the high latitudes, however, many herds of them may be ſeen in the courſe of a day's walk. The number of bulls is very ſmall in proportion to that of cows; ſo that there is every reaſon to believe they kill each other. They delight in the moſt ſtony and mountainous parts of the barren ground.

Though of conſiderable magnitude, and apparently little adapted for agility, they climb the rocks with the facility of goats; and like them, too, feed on every thing, moſs, herbage, or browſe.

The muſk ox, when full grown, is about the ordinary ſize of Engliſh black cattle; but their legs are ſhorter and thicker. The tail is ſhort, and always bent inwards, ſo that it is entirely hid in the long hair of the rump and hind quarters. The hunch on the ſhoulders is not very prominent; the hair, on ſome parts is very long, particularly on the bulls, under the throat, where it appears like a horſe's mane inverted, and gives the animal a very formidable appearance. It is of this hair that the Eſquimaux make their muſketto wigs. Towards the approach of winter, they are provided with a fine thick wool, or fur, which grows at the root of the long hair, and ſhields them from the intenſe cold of that ſeaſon, in this dreary climate. This covering of nature falls off and immediately a new one begins to appear.

The fleſh of the muſk ox reſembles that of the mooſe or elk; the fat is a clear white, ſlightly tinged with azure. The calves and young heifers are good eating; but the fleſh of the bulls ſmells and taſtes ſo ſtrong of muſk, that it is almoſt intolerable. Even the knife that cuts the fleſh of an old bull, will ſmell ſo ſtrong, that nothing but ſcowering it can remove the ſcent. The organs of generation, however, and parts adjacent, are moſt ſtrongly impregnated.

The weather being fine and moderate on the 8th, they walked about eighteen or twenty miles, and meeting with ſome deer, they kindled a fire, and made a better and more comfortable meal than they had done for a week. Their clothes too were now dried by the ſun and wind, and they felt themſelves in paradiſe, compared with their late ſituation.

That night they lay near Bear Grizzled Hill, which takes its name from the number of thoſe animals that retire hither to bring forth their young in a cave. Our author having heard ſo much of this ſpot, he had the curioſity to view it.

He found nothing, however, to reward his labour, but a tumulus of loamy earth, in the middle of a marſh. There are ſeveral little hills of the ſame kind;

but the higheſt is not more than twenty feet above the level of the ground.

On the ſide of Grizzled Bear Hill is a large cave, which penetrates a conſiderable way into the rock, and may probably have been the labour of the bears, which have made numerous deep furrows in ſearch of ground-ſquirrels and mice, which conſtitute a favourite part of their food.

The weather being very favourable on the 9th, they walked a great number of miles, and by the way ſaw plenty of deer and muſk oxen. Next day, about noon, it became ſo hot and ſultry, that walking was quite irkſome; they therefore put up on the top of a high hill, and as the moſs was then dry, they lighted a fire, and would have been comfortable in other reſpects, had not the moſchettoes ſtung them in the moſt intolerable manner.

The ſubſequent day was alſo very ſultry. After walking about ten miles, they fell in with a northern Indian leader, named Owl-Eye, and his family, in company with ſeveral Copper Indians, killing deer with bows, arrows, and ſpears. Mr. Hearne ſmoked his calumet with theſe ſtrangers, and found them much leſs ſociable than their countrymen, whom he had formerly ſeen; for though they had plenty of proviſions, they would not part with a mouthful; but on the contrary tried to rob and plunder them of every thing.

The 12th was ſo ſultry, that they did not move; but early next morning they ſet out forward, in hopes of reaching Copper-Mine River that day. However, having mounted a long chain of hills, at the foot of which they were told the river ran, they found it to be no more than a branch of it, which fell into the main ſtream about forty miles from its influx into the ſea.

At this time all the Copper Indians were diſpatched different ways, ſo that none of them knew the neareſt road. Directing their courſe, however, by the ſide of this rivulet, in hopes of coming to the main ſtream, they fell in with ſeveral fine buck deer, which they killed, and feaſted on with great glee.

After regaling themſelves, and taking a few hours reſt, they once more ſet forward, and after walking about ten miles, they arrived at the long-wiſh-for ſpot, the Copper-Mine River.

Scarcely had they arrived here, when they were joined by four of the natives with two canoes. They had ſeen all the Indians who had been ſent to announce their approach, except Matonabbee's brother and party, who had ſet out firſt.

Mr. Hearne was not only ſurpriſed, but mortified, to find the river ſo very different from the deſcriptions of it given at the factory. Inſtead of being navigable for ſhipping, as had been repreſented, it would ſcarcely ſwim an Indian canoe, being every where full of ſhoals and frequent falls.

Near the edge of the ſtream, which might be about one hundred and eighty yards broad, were ſome kinds of wood; but though it ſeemed to have been more plentiful formerly, there was very little in the vicinity, and none fit for any other purpoſe than the fire.

Soon after their arrival, three Indians were dispatched to look out for any Esquimaux who might be on the banks of the river; and every precaution was taken to prevent an alarm, that the destined victims might fall into their hands without apprehension.

On the morning of the 15th of July, Mr. Hearne began his survey, and proceeded down the river, which was every where full of shoals; and in some places vastly contracted in its breadth. Next day he advanced about ten miles farther, and found it the same.

Soon after they suspended the survey for the day, three spies returned, and reported that they had discovered five tents in the most favourable situation for a surprise. All attention to the business of the survey was now suspended; the whole thoughts of the Indians were absorbed in planning the best mode of attack, and of stealing on the poor savages, when asleep, and killing them all.

Having crossed the river in canoes, and got all the weapons in order, each painted a part of his ſhield with ſome figure, generally the ſun, moon, or ſome bird or beaſt of prey, in which they placed their reliance for ſucceſs in the intended engagement.

From the hurry in which this buſineſs was executed, and the deficiency both of ſkill and colours, moſt of the paintings had little reſemblance to any thing in heaven or on earth; but they ſatisfied the artiſts, and that was ſufficient.

This piece of ſuperſtition being completed, they advanced towards the Eſquimaux tents with the utmoſt caution and ſilence; and though an undiſciplined rabble, and by no means accuſtomed to war, no ſooner had they entered on this horrid ſcheme, than they acted with the utmoſt uniformity of ſentiment. There was neither altercation nor contending opinion; all were united in the general cauſe, and as ready to follow as Matonabbee to lead.

Never was a reciprocity of intereſt more generally regarded; and if ever the ſpirit of diſintereſted friendſhip animated the breaſt of a northern Indian, it was here diſplayed in glowing colours. Property of every kind ceaſed to be private: each was proud of an opportunity of ſupplying the wants of his neighbour.

The attacking party was judged to be quite as numerous as the Eſquimaux in their five tents, could poſſibly be; and beſides, being ſo much better equipped, nothing leſs than a miracle was likely to ſave the poor ſavages from a general maſſacre.

The land was ſo ſituated, that they walked under cover of the rocks and hills, till within two hundred yards of the tents. Here they halted, to watch the motions of the enemy, and would have perſuaded our author to remain till the engagement was over.

But though he diſclaimed having any interference in the deed of death, he thought it more prudent to accompany them; and the Indians were not a little gratified with his promptneſs to be of the party.

The laſt ceremonies were now performed, which conſiſted in painting their faces; ſome black, ſome red, and others a mixture of the two. They next made themſelves as light as poſſible for running, by almoſt ſtripping themſelves naked. Mr. Hearne, fearing he might have occaſion to run with the reſt, pulled off his ſtockings and cap, and tied up his hair as cloſely as poſſible.

It was now near one in the morning* of the 17th, when, finding the Eſquimaux all ſtill, they ruſhed from their ambuſcade, and fell on the unſuſpecting ſavages, who did not perceive their danger till it was too late to avoid it.

The ſcene was ſhocking beyond deſcription. The unhappy victims were ſurpriſed in the middle of their ſleep; men, women, and children, to the number of twenty, ran out of their tents ſtark naked, and endeavoured

* It is proper to obſerve, they were far within the arctic circle, where the ſun never ſets at this ſeaſon of the year.

to fly; but the Indians had poſſeſſion of the land ſide; and as they did not attempt to throw themſelves into the river, the whole fell a ſacrifice to unprovoked barbarity.

Their ſhrieks were moſt dreadful; but no part of this bloody affair filled our author with deeper horror than the fate of a young girl, apparently about eighteen. She was ſtabbed ſo near him, that ſhe fell down at his feet, and twiſted round his legs; ſo that he could ſcarcely extricate himſelf from her dying graſp. He ſolicited hard for her life; but the murderers made no reply till they transfixed her with two ſpears. They then looked ſternly at him, and in ridicule, aſked him if he wanted an Eſquimaux wife.

Though the poor wretch was twining round their ſpears, they continued their taunts; when Mr. Hearne begged they would at leaſt releaſe her from her miſery. On which one of them pierced her through the breaſt. The love of life, however, prompted her to attempt to ward off the blow, which, in her ſituation, was the extreme of mercy to inflict.

"My ſituation," ſays our author, "and the terror of my mind, at the ſight of this butchery, can neither be conceived nor deſcribed. Though I ſummoned up all my reſolution, it was with difficulty I could refrain from tears: even at this hour, I cannot reflect on the tranſactions of that horrid day, without the moſt painful emotions."

But the brutality of theſe ſavages, to the bodies they had deprived of life, was ſtill as ſhocking, and certainly more inexcuſable. Their indecent curioſity in examining the conformation of the women, which they pretended to ſay differed from their own, made nature revolt at the idea.

When theſe people were all maſſacred, ſeven other tents on the other ſide of the river attracted their notice; but providentially for the Eſquimaux, the baggage and canoes had been left ſome way up the river, and there was no other way of croſſing it. The river here was about eighty yards over; and to alarm them if they could not kill them, they began firing. The poor Eſquimaux, though on the watch, were ſo much unacquainted with the nature of fire-arms, that they did not attempt to fly. When the bullet ſtruck the ground, they ran with a vacant curioſity to ſee what it was. At length one of them was wounded in the leg, which immediately threw them into confuſion. They ran to their canoes, and were ſoon out of the reach of the northern Indians.

Having plundered the tents of the deceaſed of all the copper veſſels they could find, they aſſembled on the top of an adjacent hill, and forming a circle with their ſpears erect, claſhed them together, and gave many ſhouts of victory; frequently calling out tima! tima! or what cheer, by way of deriſion to the poor ſurviving Eſquimaux, who were ſtanding almoſt knee deep in the water.

After parading for ſome time, they ſet out for their canoes, and ſailing under cover of the bank, they approached the other tents, where the Esquimaux, thinking probably they were gone, had returned, and were busy in tying up bundles. These were seized, but the owners fortunately escaped again in their canoes, except one old man, who was too intent on his business, and who fell a sacrifice to their fury; for not fewer than twenty had a hand in his death.

As they were retreating from the first scene of blood, they found an old woman, sitting by the side of the river, killing salmon, which lay very thick at her feet. Whether from the noise of the fall, or a great defect in sight, she had not been apprized of the murder of her companions, though not more than two hundred yards distant from the scene of blood; nor did she discover her enemies, till they were just within reach of her.

To fly was in vain. She was pierced through with numerous spears, with the most marked and studied cruelty.

The only inſtrument that this poor half-blind wretch had to catch ſalmon with, was a light pole, armed with a few ſpikes, which ſhe put under water, and pulled up with a jerk. Some of the Indians tried this method of fiſhing; and ſo extremely numerous were the ſalmon at this place, that they ſeldom brought up leſs than two at a pull.

Theſe fiſh, though very fine and beautifully ſpotted red, were ſeldom more than about ſix or ſeven pounds weight; but their numbers were almoſt incredible, and equal to any thing related of the ſhoals in Kamſchatka. Indeed the Eſquimaux have ſcarcely any other means of ſubſiſtence than fiſh.

After having plundered the ſecond encampment, the northern Indians threw the tents into the river, and deſtroyed a large ſtock of proviſions, merely from the infernal ſatisfaction of doing all the miſchief in their power to the unhappy Eſquimaux, who were ſtanding on a diſtant ſhoal, the woful ſpectators of their loſs.

This business being completed, they refreshed themselves; and then told Mr. Hearne, that they were again ready to assist him in the survey. He therefore instantly set about it, and pursued it to the mouth of the river, which was in every part so full of shoals and falls, as not to be navigable even by a boat. The tide happened to be out, and a bar evidently obstructed the very entrance of the stream. At the estuary of the river, the sea is full of islands and shoals, as far as the telescope can reach. The ice, though it was the 17th of July, was only partially broken up round the shores.

Finding, after all his labour, that this river was unfit for being the channel of any commercial intercourse; and a thick fog and drizzling rain coming on, he did not wait to take an exact observation for determining the latitude, but immediately set out with his attendants, on his return to the southward.

However, before we proceed, it will be proper to give a more particular account of the river and the country adjacent. Befides fome ftunted pines, there are tufts of dwarf willows on the banks, plenty of what is called wifhacumpucky, fome jackafheypuck, and a few cranberries and heathberry bufhes; but not the leaft appearance of any fruit. Even this fcanty vegetation decreafes as the river approaches the fea; and for the laft thirty miles, nothing is to be feen but barren hills and marfhes, fome patches of herbage, and at the foot of the hills fine fcurvy-grafs.

The general direction of the river is nearly north by eaft, and its breadth varies from twenty to four or five hundred yards. The banks are generally a folid rock; both fides of which correfpond, and furnifh an irrefragable proofs that the channel was formed by fome violent convulfion of nature.

Some of the Indians pretend that the Copper-Mine River takes its rife from the north fide of Large White Stone Lake, which is diftant three hundred miles in a ftraight line; but our author cannot think that its ſource is ſo remote, otherwiſe he conceives its volume muſt be infinitely greater than it is.

The Eſquimaux, who reſide on this river, are rather low in ſtature, and though thick ſet, are neither well made nor ſtrong. Their complexion is a dirty copper colour, though ſome of the women are more fair. Their dreſs reſembles that of the Greenlanders in Davis's Straights, except that the women's boots are not ſtiffened out with whalebone, and the tails of their jackets are much ſhorter.

Their arms and fiſhing tackle exactly reſemble thoſe of their nation in Hudſon's Straights, but for want of edge-tools, are inferior in workmanſhip.

Their tents are made of parchment deer ſkins in the hair, and are pitched in a circular form. In winter, however, they have huts half underground, riſing and pointed like a cone: theſe are always erected in the moſt ſheltered ſituations.

Their domeſtic utenſils conſiſt of ſtone kettles and wooden troughs; diſhes, ſcoops, and ſpoons made of the horns of the muſk ox. Some of their kettles are capable of containing five or ſix gallons, and are hollowed out in the form of an oblong ſquare, with no other inſtrument than a harder ſtone to work with.

Their hatchets are made of a thick lump of copper, about five or ſix inches long, and about two inches ſquare, bevelled away like a mortice-chiſſel, with a handle about a foot, or more, in length. Neither the weight nor the ſharpneſs will admit of the tool being uſed with much ſucceſs by itſelf, and therefore it is generally applied to the wood like a chiſſel, and driven in with a heavy club.

The ſpears and knives are alſo made of copper, and among the ſpoils of twelve tents, only two ſmall pieces of iron were found.

Theſe people had a fine breed of dogs, with ſharp erect ears, ſharp noſes and buſhy tails. They were all tied to ſtones, probably to prevent them from eating the fiſh that was ſpread out to dry on the rocks. The Indians did not meddle with thoſe animals; but after they had retired, lamented they had not brought off ſome of them for uſe.

Though there appeared ſcarcely any difference between theſe people and the natives of Hudſon's Bay, in their general appearance and domeſtic economy, yet as the former had all the hair of their heads pulled out by the roots, they might ſafely be pronounced of a different tribe.

Near the mouth of the Copper-Mine River they ſaw many ſeals on the ice, and flocks of marine fowls flying about the ſhores. In the adjacent pools were alſo ſwans and geeſe in a moulting ſtate, and in the marſhes ſome curlews and plovers.

That the muſk oxen, deer, bears, wolves, foxes, alpine hares, and various other quadrupeds, are the conſtant denizens of this coaſt, is a fact that may be dependrd on. Mr. Hearne did not ſee any bird peculiar to thoſe parts, except what the Copper Indians call the Alarm Bird. It appears to be of the owl genus; and its name is ſaid to be well adapted to its qualities. When it deſcries either man or beaſt, it directs its flight towards them, and hovering over them, forms gyrations round their head. Should two objects at once arreſt their attention, they fly from the one to the other alternately, making a loud ſcreaming, like the crying of a child. In this manner they will follow travellers a whole day.

The Copper Indians have a great value for theſe birds, as they frequently indicate the approach of ſtrangers, or conduct them to the herds of deer and muſk oxen, which, without ſuch aſſiſtance, they might poſſibly miſs.

Unfortunately, however, for the Eſquimaux, they do not ſeem to place the ſame faith in the alarm bird. If they had, they muſt neceſſarily have been apprized of the approach of the northern Indians, as all the time they lay in ambuſh, before the maſſacre began, a flock of them was continually flying about, and alternately hovering over the tents of the aſſailants.

But to return. Having walked about thirty miles ſouth eaſtward of the river, they came to one of the copper mines, if it deſerves that appellation. It is no more than a jumble of rocks and gravel, which have been rent by an earthquake, and through which rolls a ſmall ſtream.

The Indians, whoſe partial accounts gave riſe to this expedition, repreſented the mine as ſo immenſely rich, that a ſhip might be ballaſted with the ore inſtead of ſtone, with perfect facility; and that the hills were entirely compoſed of that metal, all in portable lumps. After a ſearch of four hours, however, Mr. Hearne and his attendants could find only one piece of copper of any ſize, and that did not weigh more than four pounds. Yet it ſeems probable, that this metal has formerly been in much greater plenty, as the rocks and ſtones are every where tinged with verdigreaſe.

There is a ſingular tradition among the natives, that a woman firſt diſcovered thoſe mines, and that ſhe conducted her countrymen to the ſpot for ſeveral years ſucceſſively; but as ſome of them attempted to behave rudely to her, ſhe made a vow of revenge, and being a great conjurer, ſhe put it in effect. When the men had loaded themſelves with copper, ſhe refuſed to return; and ſaid ſhe would ſit on the mine till ſhe ſunk into the ground with all the copper. Next year, when the men went for their annual ſupply, ſhe had ſunk down to the waiſt, though ſtill alive, and the copper was vaſtly diminiſhed; and on their repeating their viſit the following year, ſhe had quite diſappeared, and all the principal part of the mine with her; ſo that after that period, nothing remained on the ſurface but a few ſmall pieces.*

* In this tradition the circumſtances of the copper mines appear to be ingeniouſly veiled At firſt, large lumps of metal were found on the ſurface of the earth; by degrees that was carried away; and afterwards none was to be had,

Before Churchill River was ſettled by the Hudſon's Bay Company, the northern Indians had very little iron work among them: almoſt every implement was made of copper; and to this ſpot they annually reſorted, till this metal began to fail, and they found other reſources, of a ſuperior kind. Yet to this day, the Copper Indians prefer their native ore for almoſt every uſe, except that of the hatchet, the knife, and the awl.

The Copper and Dog-ribbed Indians, lying ſo remote from the factory, generally uſe the intermediate tribes as brokers or chapmen; and in conſequence pay very dearly for every European article they ſtand in need of. Several attempts, it ſeems, have been made to induce thoſe diſtant nations to traffic immediately with the Hudſon's Bay Company, at the fort; but though

except by digging in the bowels of the earth. From our author's deſcription, there is little doubt but that there are rich mines to be found here; but of what uſe would they be, when there is no means of conveyance for the ore?

liberal presents have been given to those who had the resolution to venture so far, both for themselves and their chiefs, the northern Indians have constantly plundered them of every thing, before they could reach their homes. This hard treatment, added to the many inconveniences that attend so long a journey, are great obstacles in their way, and will ever prevent a direct and regular communication between the English and them.

Soon after they left the copper mine, a thick fog, with rain, and at intervals, heavy showers of snow, came on. This kind of weather continued for some days, and rendered their progress very slow and unpleasant.

Early on the morning of the 22d of July, they were overtaken by Matonabbee's brother and a Copper Indian. They had visited the Copper River, but met with no remarkable incident; and observing signals, which had been left for their return, they had travelled one hundred miles without stopping. The whole party immediately ſet out, and proceeded homewards upwards of forty miles that day.

The weather now became hot and ſultry; but this did not occaſion any delay in their march; and they made ſuch good uſe of their time, that, on the 24th, they reached Congecathawhachaga, where the women had been left; but, to their mortification, they found that they had croſſed the river, and were gone on.

Obſerving a great ſmoke to the ſouthward, Mr. Hearne and his party immediately proceeded towards it, and when they reached the place, they again were diſappointed; for though the women had been there a few days before, they had left it, and ſet fire to the moſs, which was ſtill burning. Their track, however, was viſible, and early on the morning of the 25th they came up with them, by the ſide of Cogead Lake.

From the time they had left the Copper-Mine River, they had travelled ſo hard and with ſo little intermiſſion, that Mr. Hearne's feet and legs were confiderably fwelled, and his ankles were become quite ftiff. The nails of his toes were likewife fo much injured, that feveral of them dropped off; and before he came up to the tents of the women, almoft every ftep was printed in blood. Even the natives began to complain; but none of them were nearly fo bad as he was.

As foon as he arrived at the women's encampment, he immediately fet about bathing and cleaning his feet; and by the affiftance of a common dreffing and reft, he was likely in a fhort time to get well. Reft, however, fo effential to his recovery, was not to be procured; for, after halting a day, the Indians refumed their march, and he was obliged to follow them.

On the 31ft they reached the fpot where the greateft number of the women, and all the children were to wait their return. Here they found feveral Indian tents; but none of Matonabbee's party had arrived. However, a fmoke being feen to the eaftward, two young men were ſent in queſt of them; and on the 5th of Auguſt, they all joined, with a number of other Indians, ſo that they now filled forty tents. Here the former huſband of one of Matonabbee's wives, who had eloped, brought her back again; but the chief had the magnanimity to take no notice of her, and bade her depart; obſerving that if ſhe had reſpected him as ſhe ought, ſhe would not have left him, and therefore ſhe was free to go where ſhe pleaſed. The woman affected concern and reluctance, though moſt aſſuredly it was not ſincere. She returned to her huſband's tent, and probably both were happy.

Several of the Indians being indiſpoſed, the conjurers, who are always the doctors, began to try their ſkill to effect their recovery. No medicine, ſave charms, is uſed for any complaint, whether external or internal. In ordinary caſes, ſucking the diſeaſed part, blowing, and ſinging to it, ſpitting, and uttering much unintelligible jargon, compoſe the proceſs of the cure.

For complaints in the bowels, it is common to ſee thoſe jugglers blowing up the anus till their eyes are almoſt ready to ſtart from their ſockets; and this operation is performed without regard to age or ſex. The accumulation of ſo large a quantity of wind is apt, at times, to occaſion ſome extraordinary emotions in the patient; and it is a laughable ſcene, in ſuch caſes, to ſee the doctor and the ſick perſon; the one blowing up wind, and the other eaſing nature, perhaps at one and the ſame moment.

When a friend, for whom they have a particular regard, is ſuppoſed to be dangerouſly ill, they occaſionally have recourſe to another very extraordinary piece of ſuperſtition, namely ſwallowing hatchets, knives, or the like.

On theſe occaſions a conjuring houſe is erected, by driving the ends of four ſmall poles into the ground, the tops of which are tied together, and then covered with a tent cloth, with a little aperture at top to admit the light. In the middle of this tent, the patient is laid; and ſometimes five or ſix conjurers, quite naked, enter; and ſecuring the door, kneel round the ſick, and begin to ſuck and blow the part affected. After a ſhort proceſs of this kind, they ſing and talk as if converſing with familiar ſpirits, which they pretend actually appear to them in the form of beaſts, or birds of prey.

Having finiſhed this ideal conference, they call for the hatchet, bayonet, or the like, which is always prepared by another perſon, and has a ſtring faſtened to one end, to aſſiſt in drawing it up again, after they have ſwallowed it; for they do not pretend to be able to digeſt, or paſs it.

Our author now ſaw an experiment of this kind. A man being dangerouſly ill, and ſome extraordinay experiments being judged neceſſary, one of the conjurers conſented to ſwallow a broad bayonet. The houſe was erected as before mentioned, the invocations took place; and the bayonet being called for, it diſappeared in the twinkling of an eye. Mr. Hearne ſays, he is not credulous enough to ſuppoſe that the juggler actually ſwallowed it; but he confeſſes, he could ſee nothing but the ſmall piece of wood at the end of the ſtring, or one ſimilar to it, between his teeth.

The juggler then paraded backward and forward for a ſhort time, when he feigned to be greatly diſordered in his ſtomach and bowels; and after many wry faces and hideous groans, by the help of the ſtring and ſome tugging, he at length produced the bayonet, apparently from his mouth, to the no ſmall ſurpriſe of the ſpectators. He then looked round with an air of exultation, and retiring into the conjuring houſe, renewed his incantations, which he continued without intermiſſion for the ſpace of twenty-four hours.

Our author admits he was not able to detect the deception, more particularly as it was performed by a naked man; and the natives themſelves ſeemed to exult at this triumph, as they ſuppoſed it, over his former incredulity. The ſick man ſoon recovered; and in a few days they proceeded to the ſouth-weſt; while the greateſt part of the ſtranger Indians left them.

On the 19th, they reached the ſide of Large White Stone Lake, which is about forty miles long. This is ſuppoſed by ſome to be the ſource of the Copper-Mine River; a circumſtance which Mr. Hearne can neither verify nor contradict.

They found deer plentiful the whole way; and many were killed for the ſake of their ſkins only. The great deſtruction which is annually made among theſe animals is almoſt incredible; yet there appears no diminution of their numbers; but in ſome places, they are even ſaid to be more plentiful than formerly.

It requires the prime part of eight or ten deer ſkins, to make a complete ſuit of clothes for a grown perſon, during winter; and all muſt be procured in the month of Auguſt, or early in September, elſe the hair will drop off with the ſlighteſt injury.

Beſides the ſkins with the hair on, each perſon wants ſeveral others to be dreſſed in leather, for ſtockings, ſhoes, and light ſummer clothing. Several more are alſo employed in a parchment ſtate to make thongs, or netting, for various purpoſes; ſo that each individual expends, in the courſe of a year, upwards of twenty deer ſkins, in clothing and other domeſtic uſes, excluſive of tent clothes and bags.

Indeed, during winter, the ſpare ſkins produce a number of warbles, which the natives pick out and eat as common food. Some of them are as large as the joint of a finger; and the children, in particular, are very fond of them. Mr. Hearne ſays, that, except theſe warbles and body lice, he has taſted of every diſh in uſe among the natives; but though he did not pretend to be over delicate, he never could bring himſelf to eat them.

The deer in thoſe regions, are indeed generally in motion from eaſt to weſt, or from weſt to eaſt, according to the ſeaſon, and the prevailing winds.

This is the principal reaſon why the northern Indians are always ſhifting their ſtations; for as deer are their chief food, and their ſkins are indiſpenſable, it is impoſſible for them to exiſt long at a diſtance from their game.

After leaving Stone White Lake, they proceeded to the ſouth-weſt, at the rate of about twelve miles a day; and, on the 3d of September, arrived at a ſmall river connected with Point Lake. Here the weather was ſo boiſterous, that it was ſome days before they could venture to croſs it in their canoes; but the time of the Indians was not loſt by this interruption, as they killed numbers of deer, as well for their ſkins as their fleſh.

In the afternoon of the 7th, they paſſed the river, and ſhaped their courſe by the ſide of Point Lake to the north-weſt. After three days eaſy journeys, they came to a ſcrubby wood, which was the firſt of any magnitude they had ſeen for upwards of three months.

One of the Indian women, who had been ſome time in a lingering ſtate, was now become ſo weak as to be incapable of travelling, which, among thoſe people is the moſt deplorable ſituation to which a human being can be reduced. No expedients were tried for her recovery, whether for want of friends, or from the ſuppoſed inability of it, is unknown; and ſhe was inhumanly left, unaſſiſted, to her fate.

This, it appears, is a common practice, ſhocking as it is; and they juſtify it by ſaying, that it is better to leave one who is paſt recovery, than for the whole family to ſit down and ſtarve in the ſame place. On ſuch occaſions, however, the friends, or the relations of the ſick, generally leave ſome victuals and water, and often a little firing, with plenty of deer ſkins. They then walk away crying, without mentioning the road they mean to purſue.

Inſtances have occurred of ſuch deſerted perſons recovering, and regaining their friends. The poor woman, juſt mentioned, thrice came up to the party; but at laſt her ſtrength totally failed her—ſhe dropped behind, and was noticed no more.

A cuſtom ſo unnatural is not often found among the human race; but the northern Indians are certainly not the only ſavages in this reſpect; and they have a better excuſe, from the neceſſity they are under to be active during the favourable ſeaſon, than any other people who are guilty of this violation of all ſocial feeling.

The early part of September gave indications that winter was approaching; and being now got among the woods, the Indians purpoſed halting for ſome time, to dreſs their ſkins for winter clothing, and to furniſh themſelves with tent poles, ſnow ſhoes, and temporary ſledges.

Towards the middle of the month, the weather became more mild and open, and continued ſo for ſeveral days; but they had almoſt inceſſant rain. On the 28th, the wind ſhifted to the north-weſt, and blew ſo cold, that in two days all the lakes and ſtanding waters were frozen over, hard enough to bear them without danger.

October commenced with heavy falls of ſnow and much drift. On the 6th, the wind blew with ſo much violence as to overſet ſeveral of the tents, and among the reſt, that in which Mr. Hearne lodged. By this misfortune, his quadrant, though well ſecured, was ſo much damaged as to be entirely uſeleſs; and he, therefore, divided its fragments among the Indians.

On the 23d, ſeveral Copper and Dog-ribbed Indians arrived at the tents, as it appeared, by previous appointment, and ſold their furs for ſuch articles of iron as the northern Indians had in their poſſeſſion. One of the Indians in Mr. Hearne's party, got forty beavers' ſkins, and ſixty martins', for a ſingle piece of iron, which he had found means to purloin the laſt time he viſited the fort.

One of the ſtrangers brought forty beaver ſkins, with which he intended to pay Matonabbee an old debt; but one of the other Indians ſeized the whole, notwithſtanding he knew for whom they were deſigned; and this irritated the chief ſo much, that he renewed his reſolution of retiring to the Athapuſco Indians. Our author did not now much interfere in his determination, though he told him that he thought ſuch behaviour uncivil, eſpecially in a man of his rank and dignity; but he diſcovered afterwards, that they all intended to take a hunting expedition into that country, for the ſake of the mooſe and the beaver, which are either very ſcarce, or never ſeen in the northern Indian territories.

Indeed, except a few martins, wolves, quick-hatches, foxes, and otters, are the chief furs to be met with in thoſe parts; and, out of ſome ſuperſtitious notion, few of the northern Indians chuſe to kill either the wolf or the quick-hatch, which they ſuppoſe to be more than common animals.

By the end of October, all their clothes and winter implements were ready, and they once more began to move. From the 1ſt to the 5th of November they walked over the ice of a large lake, which as it had no appellation before, our author called No Name Lake. This ſheet of water, or rather of ice, as it then was, is about fifty miles long and thirty-five broad. It is ſaid to abound with fine fiſh; and in the ſtate it then was, the Indians caught ſome fine trout and perch.

Having paſſed this lake, they ſhaped their courſe to the ſouth-weſt, and on the 10th reached the commencement of the main woods, when they prepared their proper ſledges, and proceeded again to the ſouth-weſt. No game was killed for ſome time, except a few partridges; however, they had by no means exhauſted their ſtock of proviſions.

After paſſing Methy Lake, and walking near eighty miles on a ſmall river that iſſues from it, on the 20th they reached Indian Lake. This piece of water, though not more than twenty miles over, is celebrated for producing plenty of fine fiſh even in winter; and accordingly the Indians ſet their nets with ſuch ſucceſs, that in about ten days they laded the women's ſledges with roes only. Tittimeg, barbel, and pike were the only fiſh they caught here. Two pounds weight of roes, well bruiſed, will make four gallons of excellent ſoup, very pleaſant to the eye, as well as the palate.

The land round this lake is very hilly, and conſiſts chiefly of looſe ſtones and rocks. However, there are ſome parts well clothed with poplars, pines, fir, and birch. Rabbits were ſo plentiful here, that ſeveral of the Indians caught twenty or thirty in a night with ſnares; and wood partridges were no leſs numerous in the trees. The fleſh of the latter is generally black and bitter, from their feeding on the bruſh of the fir tree.

During their ſtay at Indian Lake, a man being entirely palſied on one ſide, the doctors, or rather conjurers, ſet about curing him; and the perſon who had ſwallowed a bayonet in the ſummer, now offered to ſwallow a piece of board, as large as a barrel ſtave, for his recovery.

After the uſual preparatory ceremonies, the board was delivered to the conjurer, who apparently ſhoved one-third of it down his throat, and then walked round the company, continuing to ſwallow it, till no part was viſible, except a ſmall piece of the end.

As our author had doubted the former trial of his ſkill, the Indians to cure his unbelief, gave him the moſt favourable ſtation for ſeeing the exploit performed; but ſtill, though he could not be convinced of what was in itſelf impoſſible, he was unable to detect the impoſition.

Soon after, being queſtioned as to his opinion of the performance, as he was unwilling to offend by owning his ſentiments that it was a juggle, he only hinted at the impoſſibility of ſwallowing a piece of wood longer than the man's whole back, and twice as wide as his mouth. On this ſome of them laughed at him for his ignorance: and ſaid, that the ſpirits in waiting ſwallowed, or otherwiſe conveyed a-way, the ſtick, and only left the forked end apparently ſticking out of the conjurer's mouth. Matonabbee, tho' a man of ſenſe and obſervation, was ſo bigotted to the reality of thoſe feats, that he aſſured Mr. Hearne he had ſeen a man ſwallow a child's cradle with as much eaſe as he could fold up a piece of paper and put it in his mouth.

Though they pretend that the whole is done by the intervention of ſpirits, and that each conjurer has his familiar to aſſiſt him, who appears in various forms, there can be no doubt of the deception; but ſtill it is admirably performed.

As ſoon as the conjurer had finiſhed the ſwallowing remedy, five other men and an old woman, all proficients in the art, ſtripped quite naked, and entered with him into the conjuring houſe, where they began to ſuck, blow, ſing, and dance round the poor paralytic; and continued this farce for three days and as many nights, without intermiſſion, or taking the leaſt refreſhment.

At laſt, when they came out, their mouths were quite parched and black, and they were not able to articulate a ſingle ſyllable. They laid themſelves on their backs with their eyes fixed, as if in the agonies of death; and for the firſt day were treated like young children, by being fed by hand.

The paralytic, however, had not only recovered his appetite, but was able to move all the fingers and toes of the ſide that had been ſo long dead. In three weeks he could walk; and at the end of ſix went a hunting for his family. After that he accompanied Mr. Hearne to the fort, and frequently viſited the factory during the following years. But his nature ſeemed quite changed; for from being lively, benevolent, and good-natured, he became penſive, quarrelſome, and diſcontented; and never recovered the look of health.

Though the reality of the deception performed by the Indian conjurers muſt be unqueſtionable, the apparent good effects of their charms on the ſick and diseased, can only be accounted for on the principle of faith in the patient, which sets the mind at ease, and inspires hope, so essential to the well-being of man.

As a proof of the implicit confidence which is placed in the supernatural powers of these jugglers, even the threat of revenge on any person that has offended them is often fatal. The very idea that the conjurer possesses the means of destruction, preys on the spirits of the unhappy victims of his ill-will, and soon brings on a disorder that terminates his existence. A whole family has some times sunk into the grave, merely from the fancied dread of a conjurer's resentment.

Mr. Hearne says, the natives always thought him possessed of this art; and, accordingly, he was once solicited to kill a man, who had offended a chief, and who was then several hundred miles off. To please his friend, he drew some rude figures on a bit of paper, and gave it to the Indian, who wished for the destruction of his enemy. But what was our author's ſurpriſe to hear the next year, that the man, who was then in perfect health, being acquainted with his deſign againſt him, almoſt immediately ſickened, and died. He was frequently afterwards importuned to execute revenge on others; but having once eſtabliſhed his character by this fatal inſtance of Indian credulity, he never complied, in future, with ſuch requeſts. However, this gained him credit with the natives, and ſerved to keep them in awe, when he was afterwards chief of the fort.

They left Indian Lake on the 1ſt of December, and directing their courſe to the ſouthward, they arrived on the north ſide of the great Athapuſco Lake, on the 24th. In their way they ſaw many deer and beaver, plenty of which the Indians killed. The days now were ſo ſhort, that the ſun only took a circuit of a few points of the compaſs above the horizon; but the brilliancy of the aurora borealis and the ſtars, even without the aſſiſtance of the moon, made ſome amends for that deficiency, and were ſufficient to enable them to hunt the beaver, though not the deer or mooſe.

In the high northern latitudes, every variation of the colour or poſition of the aurora borealis is attended with a ruſtling and crackling noiſe, like the waving of a large flag in a freſh gale of wind. As this phenomenon is ſolved on the principle of electricity, it is ſufficient to notice it, to make it intelligible to the ſcientific.

Indian deer, as they are called, the only ſpecies found in theſe parts, except the mooſe, are vaſtly larger than thoſe which frequent the barren grounds in the territories of the northern Indians. Their hair is of a ſandy red colour during winter; their horns, though ſtronger, are leſs branching than the other kind; and their fleſh is more coarſe, but ſtill excellent food.

The beaver, however, was here the grand object of the Indians' attention, both on account of its fleſh and fur. Much as Europeans have heard about this animal, which according to ſome, is almoſt a rational being, Mr. Hearne has ſet the public right in various particulars reſpecting it; and detected the ignorance, or intentional falſity, of other writers on this ſubject, in numerous inſtances.

He ſays, the ſituation of the beaver houſes is various. Where theſe animals are very plentiful, they are found to inhabit lakes, ponds, and rivers, as well as the narrow creeks which connect the lakes. In general, however, they prefer the rivers and creeks, on account of the advantage of the current, to float the materials for their habitations.

Such as build their houſes in ſmall rivers and creeks, which are liable to become dry, ſhew an admirable inſtinct in providing againſt this calamity, by throwing a dam quite acroſs the ſtream; and in nothing do they ſhew more ability and foreſight than in this, whatever ſagacity ſome are ready to allow them.

These dams are constructed of drift wood, green willows, birch, and poplar, mud and ſtones, or whatever materials can moſt readily be procured. Their houſes are alſo made of ſimilar articles, and always proportioned in ſize to the number of inhabitants, which ſeldom exceed four old, and ſix or eight young ones. It is a miſtake, however, to ſay, that they have different apartments for their neceſſary conveniences; all that the beaver ſeems to aim at, is to have a dry place to lie on.

It, indeed, frequently happens, that ſome of the large houſes have one or more partitions; but between the inhabitants of theſe, no more than a ſocial intercourſe is kept up; nor have they any common communication but by water.

The accounts we read, in ſome books, reſpecting the manner in which the beavers build their houſes and dams, Mr. Hearne aſſures us, are mere fictions. They can neither drive piles, wattle their buildings, ſaw trees, nor uſe their tails as a trowel. Yet their ſagacity is not ſmall; and they perform all that can be expected from animals of their ſize and ſtrength.

Their work is entirely executed in the night, and they are ſo expeditious in completing it, that our author ſays, he has frequently been aſtoniſhed to ſee the quantity of mud they had collected in one night, or the progreſs they had made in a dam or houſe.

The chief food is a root reſembling a cabbage ſtalk, which grows at the bottom of lakes and rivers, and which is acceſſible to them at all ſeaſons. They are alſo fond of the bark of trees during the ſummer, and ſuch kinds of herbage and berries as the vicinity ſupplies.

When the ice breaks up in the ſpring, the beavers quit their habitations, and rove about during the ſummer, probably in queſt of a more favourable ſituation; but if they cannot ſuit themſelves better, they return to their old habitations ſoon enough to lay in their winter ſtock of woods.

Notwithſtanding what has been repeatedly reported, in regard to their forming towns and commonwealths, Mr. Hearne ſays he is confident, that even where the greateſt number of beavers are aſſembled together, their labours are not carried on jointly, nor have they any mutuality of intereſts, except in ſupporting the dam, which is common to ſeveral houſes. In ſuch caſes they have, no doubt, ſagacity enough to ſee that what is of utility to all, ſhould be repaired by the labours of each.

The beaver is capable of keeping a long time under water; ſo that when their houſes are broken up, and their retreats cut off, they generally retire to the vaults in the banks, as their laſt reſource; and here the greateſt number of them are taken.

In winter they are very fat and delicious eating, and their furs are very valuable; but in ſummer, during the breeding time, and when they are roving about, neither their fleſh nor their ſkins are of much conſequence. They produce from two to five young at a time; and though ſeveral varieties of them are mentioned, it is moſt probable, that the difference of ſeaſon alone occaſions the apparent diſtinction.*

The beaver is a remarkably cleanly animal; and is capable of being, in a great meaſure domeſticated. Mr. Hearne kept ſeveral of them, that anſwered to their names, and followed him and fondled on him like dogs. He had a houſe built for them, and a ſmall piece of water before the door, into which they always plunged when they wanted to eaſe nature. In winter they lived on the common food of the natives, and were remarkably fond of rice and plum pudding. They would even eat partridges and veniſon freely; and were the conſtant attendants on the Indian women and children, for whom they ſhewed a great partiality, and were always uneaſy in their abſence.

* Linnæus deſcribes three ſpecies of beavers, which appear to be diſtinct.

After appropriating ſeveral days to hunting beaver, they proceeded acroſs the Athapuſco Lake, in the beginning of January 1772, and arrived on the ſouth ſide of it on the 9th. From the beſt information, this lake appears to be about one hundred and twenty leagues long, from eaſt to weſt, and twenty wide, from north to ſouth. It is full of iſlands, moſt of which are clothed with trees, and ſtocked with Indian deer.

This lake produces vaſt quantities of fiſh, ſuch as pike, trout, perch, barbel, tittameg, and methy: the two laſt ſpecies of fiſh are peculiar to this country, and the ſhees, a fiſh reſembling a pike, to this lake only.

The trout here weigh commonly from thirty-five to forty pounds. Pike are alſo of an incredible ſize.

On reaching the ſouth ſide of this lake, they found the ſcene very agreeably altered. Inſtead of an entire jumble of rocks and hills, they entered on a fine champaign country, where ſcarcely a ſtone was to be ſeen.

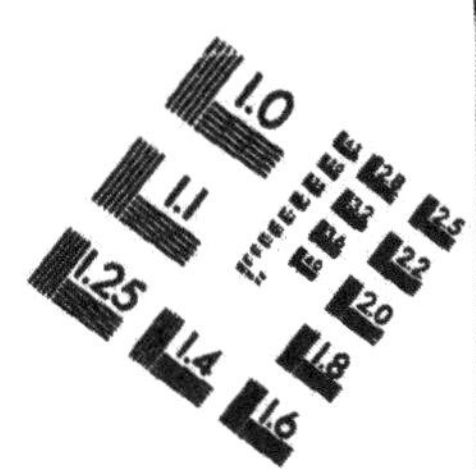

IMAGE EVALUATION
TEST TARGET (MT-3)

6"

Buffalo, mooſe, and beaver were very abundant; and in many places they could diſcover the tracks of martins, foxes, quickhatches, and other animals of the fur kind. The three former animals, however, were the ſole objects of the Indians purſuit, perhaps principally on account of the excellency of their fleſh.

The buffaloes appear much larger than the Engliſh black cattle, particularly the bulls. Their ſkin is of an incredible thickneſs, particularly about the neck; the horns are black, ſhort, and almoſt ſtraight, but very thick at the baſe. The tail is only about a foot long; and the hair of the body is ſoft and curled, generally of a ſandy brown colour.

The fleſh of this animal is entirely free from any diſagreeable ſmell or flavour, and is equal to the fineſt beef. The hunch is reckoned a very delicate bit. The tongue alſo is much eſteemed.

The mooſe deer often exceeds the largeſt horſe, both in height and bulk; but the length of the legs, the ſhortneſs of the neck, and the diſproporti-onate ſize of the head and ears, give them a very awkward appearance; and prevent them from grazing on level ground like other animals. In ſummer, they browſe on the tops of large vegetables, and the leaves of trees; and in winter, they ſubſiſt entirely on the ſmall branches of the willow and birch trees.

They are the moſt inoffenſive of all animals, and never attempt reſiſtance. It is nothing unuſual for an Indian to paddle his canoe up to one of them, and take it by the poll without oppoſition. They are eaſily tamed; and Mr. Hearne ſays, he has ſeen ſome of them that would follow their keeper, and in every thing obey his voice.

The fleſh of the mooſe is good, tho' rather coarſer and tougher than other veniſon. The noſe and tongue are peculiar delicacies. All the external fat is ſoft, and when put into a bladder, is as fine as marrow.

In all its actions and attitudes, the mooſe appears very uncouth; its gait is ſhambling, and it is both tender footed and ſhort winded. The ſkin makes excellent tent-covers and ſhoe-leather, and is dreſſed for various other purpoſes.

On the 11th of January, as ſome of the Indians were engaged in hunting, they diſcovered the track of a ſtrange ſnow ſhoe, and tracing it, they came to a little hut, where they found a young woman alone. She proved to be one of the weſtern Dog-ribbed Indians, who had been taken priſoner by thoſe of Athapuſco, in the ſummer of 1770, and had eloped from them the following ſeaſon, when they were in the vicinity, with an intention of returning to her own country; but the diſtance being ſo great, ſhe had forgot the track, and had therefore, built a hut for her protection, in which ſhe had lived about ſeven moons, without ſeeing a human face.

During this time ſhe had ſupported herſelf by ſnaring partridges, rabbits, and ſquirrels. That ſhe had not been in want was evident from her appearance, and the ſtock of proviſions ſhe had ſtill by her. Of a real Indian, ſhe was one of the fineſt women, in our author's opinion, of any he ever ſaw.

She had ſhewn infinite ingenuity in procuring a livelihood. When the few deer ſinews ſhe had carried off with her, were all expended in making ſnares, and ſewing her clothes; ſhe had uſed thoſe of the legs of rabbits with much dexterity and ſucceſs. Of the ſkins of thoſe animals, ſhe had likewiſe made herſelf a complete and neat ſuit of winter clothes; and it was evident, ſhe had extended her care beyond mere comfort, as her dreſs exhibited no little variety of ornament.

Her leiſure hours had been employed in twiſting the inner rind of willows into ſmall lines, of which ſhe intended to make a fiſhing net. Five or ſix inches of an iron hoop ſerved her for a knife, and this, together with an awl of the ſame metal, were all the implements in her poſſeſſion. She lighted a fire by rubbing two hard ſulphereous ſtones againſt each other, and when a few ſparks were produced, ſhe had touchwood ready to receive them.

The comelineſs of her perſon, and her approved accompliſhments, occaſied a ſtrong conteſt among the party, who ſhould have her to wife; and ſhe was actually won and loſt by almoſt ten men the ſame evening. Matonabbee, though he had no leſs than ſeven, women grown, and a young girl about twelve years old, wiſhed to put in his claim for her: but one of his wives ſhamed him from this, by obſerving, that he had women enough already. This piece of ſatire, however true it might be, irritated the chief ſo much, that he fell upon the poor creature, and bruiſed her ſo exceſſively, that after lingering ſome time, ſhe eſcaped from his tyranny and life.

It appeared that when the Athapuſco Indians ſurpriſed the friends of the young woman, they had butchered them all, except herſelf and three other women. Among the victims of their barbarity were her father, mother, and huſband. She had a child about four months old, which ſhe concealed in a bundle of clothing, and carried with her; but when they joined the Athapufco women, one of them fnatched it from her, and killed it on the fpot. Her new hufband, fhe faid, was remarkably fond of her, and kind to her; but this piece of barbarity fhe could never forget, and took the firft opportunity of eloping from the murderers of her infant. Affecting as this ftory was, and told at the fame time with correfpondent feeling, Mr. Hearne fays, his party only laughed at it, and turned it into ridicule.

Continuing their courfe to the fouthweft, on the 16th they arrived at the Grand Athapufco River, at a place where it was about two miles wide. The furrounding woods were very luxuriant; and the banks of the river were nearly one hundred feet above the ordinary level of the water. The foil was rich and loamy, and fome of the pines that grew here, were large enough to make mafts for fhips of the firft rate. In the river are feveral iflands, much frequented by the moofe deer.

Agreeably to Matonabbee's propoſal, they continued their march up this river for many days, in hopes of falling in with ſome of the natives; but tho' they ſaw ſeveral of their former encampments, they did not diſcover one of the people. Thus diſappointed in their expectations, it was reſolved to ſpend as much time in hunting the mooſe, buffalo, and beaver, as could be allowed, conſiſtent with their purpoſed return to the fort, by the uſual period of the ſhips' arrival from England.

Accordingly, on the 27th of January, they directed their courſe to the eaſtward; but as game was very plentiful, they made frequent halts.

About the middle of February, they walked along a ſmall river, which empties itſelf into Lake Clowey, where they had built their canoes the year before. On the 24th, they were joined by a northern Indian leader and his followers, who preſented Matonabbee and our author, with ſome roll tobacco and about two quarts of brandy. The tobacco was very acceptable, as their ſtock of that article had been long expended.

As this vicinity abounded in game, many days were ſpent in hunting, feaſting, and preparing ſuch a quantity of fleſh, as might ſerve them for ſome time; well knowing, from experience, that a few days walk farther to the eaſtward, would deprive them of the living animals.

The ſtrangers who had left the fort, about November 1771, ſoon proceeded on their journey to the north-weſtward, except a few who had been lucky in hunting, and reſolved to accompany them back to the factory, to diſpoſe of their furs.

On the laſt day of February, they reſumed their journey; and ſoon after the Indians fell in with a party of poor inoffenſive people, whom they plundered of all they had, and even carried off ſome of their young women. Theſe repeated acts of violent and unprovoked aggreſſion, ſerved to increaſe our author's indignation; and he felt very fenfibly for this in particular, as it was committed on a fet of harmlefs creatures, who were almoft fecluded from all other human fociety.

It appeared that for upwards of a generation, one family only, as it may be called, had taken up their winter abode in thofe woods; which are fo much out of the ufual track of the other Indians, as to be very feldom vifited by them. The fituation, however, was moft favourable for game of every kind, at the different feafons; but the general dependence was on fifh and partridges. Thefe advantages had tempted this fimple race to take up their abode here; feveral hundred miles from the reft of their tribe.

By the 1ft of March they began to leave the level country of the Athapufcos, and to approach the ftony mountains, which bound the northern Indian country. On the 14th, they difcovered the tracks of more ftrangers, and next day came up with them. Among them was a perfon who had carried a letter from Mr. Hearne to Prince of

Wales Fort, about a year before; and now accidentally met him, and returned an anſwer, dated in June 1771.

Theſe Indians having obtained a few furs, joined their party, which now conſiſted of about two hundred perſons. Our author found great reaſon to lament the loſs of his quadrants, as he was unable to aſcertain diſtances and ſituations, however deſirable it would have been both for curioſity and information, in a country which no other European ever traverſed.

On the 19th, they took up their lodgings near Large Pike Lake, which they croſſed next day, where it was not more than ſeven miles wide. The ſubſequent day they paſſed Bedodid Lake, which is about forty miles long and only three broad; ſo that it has the appearance of a river. The Indians ſaid it was ſhut up on all ſides by high lands, covered with pines of vaſt magnitude, compared to which, the European firs are only like fruit trees.

The thaws now commenced, and from the latter end of March to the middle of April, they were conſiderable about noon; but it commonly froze at night, and walking was by no means pleaſant. The mooſe deer now began to become very ſcarce. On the 12th of April, they ſaw ſeveral ſwans flying to the northward, which being birds of paſſage, were conſidered as the harbingers of ſpring.

On the 14th, they pitched their tents on Theelee-aza' River, where they found ſome families of ſtrange northern Indians, employed in ſnaring deer; and ſo poor, that they had not a gun among them. The villains, however, in our author's party, ſo far from adminiſtering to them relief, robbed them of every uſeful article, and abuſed ſome of their young women in a manner too ſhocking to mention, in ſpite of all the remonſtrances he could make.

Deer being plentiful near this ſpot, they halted here ten days, in order to prepare and dry a quantity of the fleſh to carry with them.

The thaw now was ſo conſiderable that ſome bare land appeared; and the ice on the ſtreams began to break up.

On the 25th, as the weather was very inviting, they again ſet out; but on the 1ſt of May, a heavy fall of ſnow came on, attended with a bitter gale of wind, which increaſed to ſuch a degree, that they were incapable of ſtanding upright, and the cold was extremely piercing.

The ſecond proved fine with warm ſunſhine; and having dried their wet clothes, they proceeded to the place where it was intended to build their canoes; but in conſequence of a diſpute between Matonabbee and ſome of his countrymen, he determined to travel farther to the eaſtward before they ſet about this neceſſary duty.

For ſome days the weather was hot and pleaſant. On the 6th, they fell in with ſome ſtrange Indians, who were proceeding to the factory with their furs; and on the invitation of Matonabbee, they joined company.

After a reſt of four days, it was agreed on to leave the elderly people and young children here, in the care of ſome Indians, till the return of their relations from the fort. Matters being thus ſettled, they ſet out on the 11th, at a much briſker pace than before; and in the afternoon of the ſame day, overtook ſome more Indians laden with furs.

The 12th was ſo warm, and the water ſo deep on the top of the ice, as to render walking on it, not only unpleaſant, but dangerous. It was, therefore, found neceſſary to conſtruct their canoes without delay; and this buſineſs being accompliſhed by the 18th, they proceeded through ſwamps of mud, water, and wet ſnow, which froze to their ſtockings and ſhoes in ſuch large cruſts, as to render travelling very laborious, and to expoſe them to the danger of having their limbs froſt-bitten.

The weather, on the 21ſt, was ſo ſharp, that the ſwamps and ponds were once more frozen over; and they found it tolerable walking. This day ſeveral Indians turned back for want of proviſions; which now began to run ſcarce, and no new ſupplies were to be found, except a few geeſe.

The following day they had the good fortune to kill two deer; but the party was now ſo large, that four of the northern deer were not more than adequate to a ſingle meal.

On the 25th, ſeveral more of the Indians abandoned the journey, for fear of famine; and as they travelled hard for ſome days, all heavy laden, and in great diſtreſs for want of food. ſome of them became too weak to carry their furs any farther, and many others, being deſtitute of guns and ammunition, were no longer capable of bearing them company.

Mr. Hearne, indeed, had plenty of both, but ſelf-preſervation obliged him to reſerve it for the uſe of his immediate attendants; eſpecially as geeſe and other birds were the only game they had to expect till they reached the fort.

The 26th was fine and pleaſant; and after walking about five miles, they fell in with and killed three deer, which, as their numbers were conſiderably leſſened, ſerved them for two or three meals, with little expence of ammunition.

They croſſed Cathawhachaga river on the 30th of May, on the ice, which broke up ſoon after the laſt party left it. Symptoms of bad weather now appeared; and it was not long before the rain deſcended in torrents, and obliged them, in the middle of the night, to retire for ſecurity to the top of an adjacent hill, where the violence of the wind would not permit them to erect their tents. In this dreary ſituation, they remained till the 3d of June, without the leaſt refreſhment; in the courſe of which time the wind ſhifted all round the compaſs, and they changed their poſition with it.

On the 4th, the ſtorm abated; and hunger compelled them to advance, wet and exhauſted as they were. In the courſe of that day's journey they killed ſome geeſe, but barely ſufficient to keep them from ſtarving.

On the 8th, however, they were fortunate enough to kill five deer, which put them all in high ſpirits; and from the numbers they ſaw, they began to indulge the hopes that more plentiful times awaited them, during the remainder of their journey.

On the 9th, as they were continuing their courſe in the direction of the factory, they ſaw ſeveral ſmokes, and ſpoke with different parties of northern Indians; but anxious to get on, they did not loſe much time in converſation.

For many days after, they found plenty of proviſions; and as the weather was remarkably fine and pleaſant, their circumſtances were vaſtly altered for the better; and they almoſt forgot their former ſufferings. The thoughts too of approaching the fort gave them new reſolution, and moderate difficulties were overlooked.

On the 18th, they arrived at Egg River, from whence Mr. Hearne diſpatched a letter to the chief at Fort

Prince Wales, to inform him of his being ſo far advanced. Here they halted a day to prepare food to carry with them.

Early on the morning of the 26th they arrived at Seal River; but the wind blew ſo ſtrong, that they could not venture to croſs it in their little canoes, before the afternoon.

On the 28th, as they were croſſing Po-co-thee-kis-co River, they were joined by ſome Indians from Fort Churchill, who brought them a little tobacco; and next morning they had the ſatisfaction to arrive ſafe at Fort Prince Wales, after an abſence of eighteen months and twenty days.

" Though my diſcoveries" ſays Mr. Heare, " are likely to prove of any material advantage to the nation at large, or, indeed, to the Hudſon's Bay Company, yet I had the pleaſure to think, that I had fully executed the inſtructions I received; and that this journey has put an end to all diſputes reſpecting a North-weſt Paſſage through Hudſon's Bay. It will alſo wipe off the ill-ground-ed and unjuſt aſperſions of ſome voyagers and travellers, thrown on the Hudſon's Bay Company, as being averſe to diſcoveries in this quarter."

We ſhall now conclude this very intereſting journey with ſome additional remarks on the northern Indians.

In their perſons they are generally above the middle ſize, well proportioned, ſtrong, and robuſt; but are leſs volatile and active than ſome of the other Indian tribes. Their complexion is of a dark copper caſt; their hair black, long, and ſtraight; and few of the men have naturally any beard, and what they have they carefully extirpate.

Their peculiar features are very low foreheads, ſmall eyes, high cheek bones, Roman noſes, full cheeks, and in general long broad chins. Their ſkin is ſoft and poliſhed, and when they are clean dreſſed, they are quite free from any offenſive ſmell. They mark their cheeks with three or four parallel black ſtrokes, which is performed by running a needle under the ſkin, and rubbing powdered charcoal into the wound.

Moroſe and covetous, the name of gratitude is ſcarcely known among them. They ſeem to take a pleaſure in enumerating their wants, even where they have no proſpect of having them relieved; and frequently laugh at the dupes of their inſincerity.

Harſh, uncourteous uſage ſeems to agree better with them than kindneſs; for if the leaſt reſpect be ſhewn them, they become intolerably inſolent. Yet as in all countries and among all people, there are ſome who are capable of eſtimating indulgence without treſpaſſing too far.

To defraud the Europeans, and to overreach them in trade, are their pleaſure and ſtudy. They diſguiſe their perſons, change their names; in ſhort, any thing to eſcape paying their lawful debts, or to enable them to contract new ones.

Notwithſtanding thoſe bad qualities, they are one of the mildeſt of the Indian tribes, the moſt ſober, and the moſt pacific.

Though jealouſy is a general paſſion among the men, marriages are contracted without ceremony, and frequently diſſolved with as little. Young women have no choice of their own. Their parents match them to the man who ſeems beſt able to maintain them, regardleſs of age, perſon, or diſpoſition.

Girls are generally betrothed, when children, to men grown up. Nor is this practice deſtitute of policy; where the very exiſtence of a family depends ſometimes on the induſtry and abilities of one man. In caſe of a father's death, the poor female children would frequently be in danger of ſtarving, did not thoſe early contracts take place, which are never violated on the part of the man, till after conſummation at leaſt.

From the age of eight or nine, girls are ſtrictly watched and cloſely confined; deprived even of innocent and cheerful amuſements, and cooped up by the ſide of old women, employed in domeſtic duties of every kind. But the conduct of the parents is by no means conſiſtent with theſe rigid reſtraints. They ſet no bounds to the freedom of their converſation before their children.

Divorces are pretty common for incontinency, bad behaviour, or even the want of ſuch accompliſhments as the huſband wiſhes to find in a wife. This ceremony conſiſts in nothing but a good drubbing, and turning the woman out of doors.

Providence has mercifully denied the woman the ſame fecundity as in more genial climes. Few produce more than five or ſix children; and theſe generally at long intervals, which enables the parents to bring them up with greater facility, than if they had ſeveral very young children to take care of at once.

For want of firing, rather than choice, theſe poor people are frequently obliged to eat their meat raw, particularly in the ſummer ſeaſon, when on

the barren ground; nor do they ever feel any inconvenience from this. Mr. Hearne ſays, he has been frequently one of a party, who has ſat down to a freſh-killed deer, and aſſiſted in picking the bones quite clean.

Their poverty is ſo great, that not many of them are able to purchaſe a braſs kettle; ſo that they are under the neceſſity of continuing their original mode of boiling their victuals in large upright veſſels, made of birch rind. As theſe will not admit of being expoſed to the fire, the defect is ſupplied by red hot ſtones, put into the water: which ſpeedily occaſion it to boil. They have various diſhes, at which the delicate ſtomach of an European would revolt.

Bows and arrows, their original weapons, are now ſuperſeded by the uſe of fire-arms, except among the very pooreſt, or when they wiſh to ſave ammunition. Deer are frequently killed during the ſummer ſeaſon with arrows; but from diſuſe, the Indians are not very dextrous in the management of thoſe weapons.

Their ſledges are of various ſizes, according to the ſtrength of the people who are to haul them. Some are not leſs than twelve or fourteen feet long, and fifteen or ſixteen inches wide; but, in general, their dimenſions are much leſs. They are compoſed of boards, a quarter of an inch thick, and about five or six inches wide, ſewed together with thongs of parchment deer ſkin. The head, or fore part, is turned up, ſo as to form a ſemicircle of about a foot and a half diameter. This prevents the ſledge from diving into light ſnow, and enables it to ſlide over the inequalities of the ſurface.

The trace, or draught line, is a double ſtring made faſt to the head; and the bight is put acroſs the ſhoulders of the hauler, ſo as to reſt againſt the breaſt, which allows the greateſt exertion of ſtrength with the leaſt toil.

Their ſnow ſhoes are ſomewhat different from the generality uſed in thoſe regions, as they muſt always be worn on one foot, the inner ſide of the frame being almoſt ſtraight, and the outſide having a large ſweep. The frames are commonly made of birch wood, and the netting is compoſed of thongs of deer ſkin.

Their clothing principally conſiſts of deer ſkin in the hair, which ſubjects them to vermin; but this is far from being conſidered as a diſgrace; and, indeed a louſy garment forms, in their eſtimation, a delicious repaſt. Diſguſting as this may appear, it is perhaps, no more indelicate than an European epicure feaſting on the mites in cheeſe.

The tract of land inhabited by the northern Indians, reaches from latitude 59 to 68 deg. and is about five hundred miles in width. The ſurface is frequently covered with a thin ſod of moſs; but, in general, it is no more than one ſolid maſs of rocks and ſtones. It produces ſome cranberries, and a few other inſignificant ſhrubs and herbage; and in the marſhes are found different kinds of graſs: but nature has been very ſparing in her gifts in the vegetable claſs.

There is a kind of moſs of a black, hard, crumply appearance, growing on the rocks and large ſtones, which is of infinite ſervice to the natives, as it ſometimes furniſhes them with a temporary ſubſiſtence, when no other food is to be procured. When boiled, it turns to a gummy conſiſtence, and is neither unpalateable nor unwholeſome. Fiſh and deer, however, conſtitute their principal ſupport; and theſe are in moſt places, ſufficiently abundant at the proper ſeaſons.

When two parties of thoſe Indians meet, they make a full halt within a few yards of each other, and, in general, ſit or lie down for a few minutes. At length one of them, commonly breaks ſilence, and when he has made his oration, the ſpeaker of the other party begins his reply.

They have few diverſions; and in a country where want can only be warded off by conſtant diligence, it is not to be expected that they ſhould ſhine in elegant amuſements. Dancing, however, is not unknown among them; and this exerciſe the men always perform naked. The women, unleſs they are commanded by their huſbands or fathers, never ſhare in it, and then always by themſelves.

A ſcorbutic eruption, conſumptions, and fluxes, are their chief diſorders. The firſt, though very troubleſome, is never of itſelf fatal; but the two latter carry off great numbers of both ſexes and all ages. Indeed, few attain to longevity, probably owing to the rigours of the climate, and the great fatigues they inceſſantly undergo. They never bury their dead, but leave them to be devoured by the birds and wild beaſts.

The death, however, of a near relation affects them moſt ſenſibly. They rend their clothes, cut their hair, and cry almoſt inceſſantly for a great length of time. The periods of mourning are regulated by moons; and they ſeem to ſympathize with each other on their reſpective loſſes, as if poſſeſſed of the fineſt ſenſibility; yet there is certainly much of habit in this, and the emotions of nature have only a partial ſhare, either in their ſorrow or condolence.

Religion, as a rule of life, has not yet begun to dawn among the northern Indians, superſtitious as they are. Yet they think and ſpeak reſpectfully of the devotion of others; and ſome of them are not unacquainted with the hiſtory of the great Author of Chriſtianity. Matonabbee, who, our author ſays, was one of the beſt informed and ſenſible men he ever knew among them, gave the following account of his countrymen.—"Their only object is to conſult their intereſt, inclinations, and paſſions; and to paſs through this world with as much eaſe and contentment as poſſible, without any hopes of reward, or painful fear of puniſhment in the next." Theſe are the ſentiments and the objects of the irreligious in all countries, however much policy may teach them to diſguiſe their thoughts.

When the aurora borealis is very bright, and varying much in form, colour, and ſituation, they ſay their deceaſed friends are very merry; but the immortality of the ſoul is by no means a general belief among the northern Indians; though their ſouthern neighbours have certainly ſome faint ideas of it. Yet they are very ſuperſtitious with reſpect to the exiſtence of ſeveral kinds of furies, whom they call Nant-e-na, and whom they pretend ſometimes to ſee. Theſe are ſuppoſed to inhabit the different elements; and to ſome one or other of them, every change in their circumſtances is uſually aſcribed.

FINIS.

Printed in the USA
CPSIA information can be obtained
at www.ICGtesting.com
LVHW012059200324
775037LV00003B/23